FOR THE LOVE OF BEING

Jewish

An A-to-Z Primer for Bubbies, Mensches, Meshugas, Tzaddiks, and Yentas!

Written by Rabbi **Steven Stark Lowenstein**   Illustrated and designed by **Mark Anderson**

If the statistics are right, the Jews constitute but one percent of the human race. It suggests a nebulous dim puff of star dust lost in the blaze of the Milky Way. Properly the Jew ought hardly to be heard of, but he is heard of, has always been heard of. He is as prominent on the planet as any other people, and his commercial importance is extravagantly out of proportion to the smallness of his bulk. His contributions to the world's list of great names in literature, science, art, music, finance, medicine, and abstruse learning are also away out of proportion to the weakness of his numbers. He has made a marvellous fight in the world, in all the ages; and has done it with his hands tied behind him. He could be vain of himself, and be excused for it.

The Egyptian, the Babylonian, and the Persian rose, filled the planet with sound and splendor, then faded to dream-stuff and passed away; the Greek and the Roman followed, and made a vast noise, and they are gone; other peoples have sprung up and held their torch high for a time, but it burned out, and they sit in twilight now, or have vanished. The Jew saw them all, beat them all, and is now what he always was, exhibiting no decadence, no infirmities of age, no weakening of his parts, no slowing of his energies, no dulling of his alert and aggressive mind. All things are mortal but the Jew; all other forces pass, but he remains. What is the secret of his immortality?

—Mark Twain *Harpers magazine, March 1898*

"A" IS FOR Abraham,

The father of us all.
He left his father's business
When he heard the famous call.

THE THREE MAIN RELIGIONS OF THE WORLD all trace their roots back to Abraham, who is considered the first Jew. Like a good son, he worked in his father's business for as long as he could. In Chapter 12 of Genesis he was told, "Lech Lecha"—go forth. He was the very first individual to believe in monotheism, the belief in one God. He had no past and no bubbly personality. He began at age 75 to cross over into a new land with his wife and nephew. He circumcised himself at age 99. He was the first to make a deal with God. Blessed with two children, he almost sacrificed his son, Isaac, and then died at the ripe old age of 175.

"I don't believe in an afterlife, although I am bringing a change of underwear." —Woody Allen

"More than Israel has kept the Sabbath, the Sabbath has kept Israel." —Ahad Ha'am

Bracha = Blessing   Bubkis = Nothing   Ba'al Tashchit = Do not destroy (protect the environment)

Bar/Bat Mitzvah = Rite of passage for 13-year-old to be called to the Torah   Bashert = Predestined

"B" IS FOR Bubala and Boychick,

Guests at the brunch table.

Mel Brooks and Ben Gurion say the bracha

Over the bagels, lox, and sable.

A BLESSING OR BRACHA is the way that we praise, thank, and/or petition God. Tradition teaches that we should try to recite at least 100 blessings per day. The recitation of blessings is a constant reminder—for every human being—of who we are and what we can hope to become. There are blessings for everything and everyone.

"Look at Jewish history. Unrelieved lamenting would be intolerable. So, for every ten Jews beating their breasts, God designated one to be crazy and amuse the breast-beaters. By the time I was five I knew I was that one." —Mel Brooks

"In order to be a realist, you must believe in miracles." —David Ben Gurion

Challah = Braided egg bread   Chesed = Kindness   Chuppah = Wedding canopy

Chutzpah = Audacity, nerve   Covenant = Agreement/brit

"C" IS FOR

Covenant,

Making God crystal clear.

They called us the "Chosen"

Giving us nothing to fear.

CHOSEN PEOPLE? According to the Bible, God entered into a covenant with Abraham and his descendants to be God's partner and emissary in the world. This concept has been distorted through the ages to mean that Jews regard themselves as God's chosen people, thus superior to other people.

In truth, this "chosenness" puts a heavy burden on the Jewish people rather than endowing them with special privileges. It requires the Jewish people to be a "Light unto the Nations." Being chosen does not mean being better than others, but rather having a special mission that requires a high moral code of conduct and responsibility. This covenant requires unshakable faith between God and the Jewish people.

"Freedom of expression is the matrix, the indispensable condition, of nearly every other form of freedom." –Benjamin Cardozo

From the first time I saw Sid Caesar be funny, I knew that's what I had to do." –Billy Crystal

Daven = To pray   Derech Eretz = Do the right thing If you want to make peace   Dreidel = Spinning top for Chanukah

"D" IS FOR David,

The mightiest of kings.
It also stands for Dylan,
The Bobby Zimmerman who sings.

DIASPORA AND DAVID: Since the destruction of the Temple in 586 BCE, the Jewish people have spread all over the world.

Today, with 12 to 14 million Jews scattered around the world making up less than one half of 1 percent of the world's population, there are

Jews everywhere from D.C. to Damascus. Yet from that exile, the Jewish people have remained a single family overcoming obstacles.

Kind David (1010–970 BCE) is the second King of Israel who arose from a young shepherd to unite the tribes of Israel and become

one of its most powerful figures. With a pebble from a small slingshot, he slew the great Goliath. He defeated the Philistines so soundly that

they were quiet for centuries. He is remembered as a great warrior and a loyal and trusted friend. The author of Psalms, David has been called

the "Sweet Singer of Israel."

"May God bless and keep you always. May your wishes all come true. May you always do for others and let others do for you.
May you build a ladder to the stars and climb on every rung. May you stay forever young." —Bob Dylan

Ein Sof = Without end   Emet = Truth   Emunah = Faith

"E" IS FOR

Exodus,

The escape from cruel oppression.
And for E=mc²,
Albert Einstein's brilliant expression.

THE SINGLE GREATEST EVENT in the history of the Jewish people is the Exodus from Egypt. From the Greek meaning "going out," in this second book of the Bible we learn the story of the Egyptian oppression, the selection of Moses, the ten plagues, the early morning departure from Egypt, God's revelation at the foot of Mount Sinai, and the giving of the Torah. It was on this journey that the Jewish people went from slavery to freedom—a freedom we continuously celebrate in every generation.

"Life is a gift, and if we agree to accept it, we must contribute in return.
When we fail to contribute, we fail to adequately answer why we are here." —Albert Einstein

"For the Jews there was great light and joy, happiness, and honor." —Esther 8:16

"F" IS FOR

Frankfurter and Fortas,

Who, through hard work, realized their dreams.
With Justices Breyer, Brandeis, Goldberg, and Ginsburg
They've become THE JEWISH SUPREMES.

IN 1916, LOUIS DEMBITZ BRANDEIS became the first Jewish Supreme Court justice, but only after a tumultuous confirmation process. The 1932 appointment of Benjamin Cardozo raised mild controversy for placing two Jewish justices on the court at the same time. Cardozo was succeeded by Felix Frankfurter in 1939, Arthur Goldberg in 1962, and Abe Fortas in 1965—each of whom filled what became known as the "Jewish Seat." In 1993 Ruth Bader Ginsburg and in 1994 Stephen Breyer were added; both highly respected Jewish justices were still serving on the highest court in the land as of 2010.

"In spite of everything, I still believe that people are really good at heart." —Anne Frank

"Why the people of Israel adhered to their God all the more devotedly the worse they were treated by him, that is a question we must leave open." —Sigmund Freud

Felix FRANKFURTER

Ruth Bader GINSBURG

Abraham FORTAS

Louis Dembitz BRANDEIS

"G" IS FOR

God

Enough said!

"God was in this place and I, I didn't know it." —**Genesis 28:16**

"The inability to hear a new revelation is one of the signs of death of the soul." —**Rabbi Yitz Greenberg**

"H" IS FOR

Who dreamt of a Jewish State,
And for Hillel and Rabbi Heschel,
Philosophers, first-rate.

AT LEAST THREE DIFFERENT TIMES IN HISTORY, individuals with the initial "H" harnessed hope

for great change. Hillel lived from 110 BCE TO 10 CE and is considered one of the most important figures in Jewish history. He is popularly

known as the author of two sayings: "If I am not for myself, who will be for me? And when I am for myself, what am I? And if not now, when?"

And "That which is hateful to you, do not do to your fellow. That is the whole Torah; the rest is explanation; go and learn." Theodore Herzl

lived from 1860–1904 and is considered the visionary of the Jewish State and the father of modern Zionism. He said, "If you will it, it is no

dream." Abraham Joshua Heschel was born in Europe in 1907 and died in the United States in 1972. He was the leading Jewish theologian and

philosopher of the 20th century. A prominent leader in civil rights, he once wrote, "When I marched in Selma, my feet were praying."

"In a place where people do not behave with humanity, strive to be human." —Hillel

Ima = Mother   Israel = One who wrestles with God   Ivree = Hebrew

"I" IS FOR Israel,

A place like no other.

It also stands for Isaac and Ishmael,

Who luckily didn't have another brother.

THE LAND OF ISRAEL, has been central to Judaism since its very beginnings. The covenant that God made with Abraham included the promise of land—which would eventually come to be known as Israel. It is a physical and spiritual homeland for the Jewish people forever. Wherever Jews live, they pray facing east—toward the holy city of Jerusalem. For almost 1,900 years, at the end of every Passover Seder, the hope and prayer, "Next Year in Jerusalem," has been uttered.

"Arise, shine, for your light has dawned and the presence of God has shone upon you." —Isaiah 60:1

"J" IS FOR Billy Joel

And Al Jolson, whose voices never fail,
And for Jesus, Jacob, Jeremiah,
And, of course, Jonah and the whale.

FROM A JEWISH PERSPECTIVE, Jesus was a great prophet and teacher from Galilee who lived at the beginning of the Common Era. The teachings and parables of Jesus and those attributed to him were so compelling they gave rise to a worldwide religion called Christianity. Jesus lived and died at a time and in a place when there was great turmoil and messianic fervor, and the stories about him can be understood against the background of an entire people yearning for salvation and redemption.

"The question is not whether we will survive, but who and how many will survive. And this will depend on the degree to which we can try and recapture the masses of our young people to the thrills of Jewish learning and Jewish living." —Immanuel Jakobovits

Kavanah = Intention   Kavod = Honor   Kibitz = Talk playfully   Kiddush = Blessing over the wine

Klutz = Especially clumsy person   Kvell = Overflowing with pride   Kvetch = Complain

"K" IS FOR

Kol Nidre,

The fast that goes slow.

But for Koufax on Yom Kippur

It was to synagogue he did go.

THE TASK OF LIVING JEWISHLY is to seek holiness in everything we say and do. The Hebrew word for holiness is kadosh (meaning "separate" or "unique")—chosen and designated from among all other similar things for special purpose or use. Kol Nidre (meaning "all vows") on the eve of Yom Kippur (the Day of Atonement) is considered by many the holiest religious observance of the Jewish year. Speaking of Kol Nidre, left-handed pitcher Sandy Koufax was the first Major League Baseball player to throw four no-hitters. In Game 1 of the 1965 World Series, Koufax chose not to pitch on Yom Kippur out of respect for his Jewish tradition. Now that is kadosh!

"To take the old and make it new and take the new and make it holy." —Abraham Isaac Kook

"L" IS FOR Emma

Lazarus,

Her poem inscribed on Liberty's "Golden Door,"
And also for Polo's Ralph Lauren,
His fancy threads in every store.

LAMED VAV TZADDIKIM—literally, 36 righteous human beings—these secret saints are the center of many stories and mystical legends. All of the tales are based on the teachings of Abbaye, a great first-century rabbi mentioned in the Talmud, a book of Jewish law. It explains there are at least 36 righteous people in the world at all times. Their identities are never known by them or anyone else. They are so pious and modest that they hide their learning and their good deeds. According to this legend, before one of the 36 dies, another is always born, saving our cruel world from destruction. Maybe you are one of them?

"Give me your tired, your poor, your huddled masses yearning to breathe free, the wretched refuse of your teeming shore. Send these, the homeless, tempest-tossed to me, I lift my lamp beside the golden door!" —Emma Lazarus

"M" IS FOR

Moses,

Who climbed a mountain quite rocky.
Another M is for Golda Meir,
The greatest export from Milwaukee.

THE TORAH CONTAINS 613 MITZVOT OR COMMANDMENTS. The most famous of the mitzvot are the Ten Commandments brought down by Moses from Mount Sinai. Engraved on two stone tablets, these famous laws address the central issues of ethical human behavior—between humans and God and between us and our fellow human beings. According to legend, Moses climbed Mount Sinai multiple times to discuss, argue, and comprehend God's covenant, a process that continues every time we study and learn.

"I find television very educating. Every time somebody turns on the set, I go into the other room and read a book." —Groucho Marx

Naches = Pride   Nes = Miracle   Nosh = Eat something light   Nu = So

"N" IS FOR Ner Tamid,

The Eternal Light so bright.

It also stands for Never Forget

As the Holocaust darkened our light. ____

"NEVER FORGET" is our obligation to both remember the victims of the Holocaust and work to ensure that no such genocide can

ever take place in any corner of our world. From 1939–1945, 6 million Jews and 12 million people in all lost their lives throughout Europe

during the Shoah, the Holocaust. Ner Tamid is the eternal light, representing God's presence, that burns continually in synagogues around the

world. We must never forget in order to keep this light burning and never allow darkness to again overtake our world.

"The whole wide world is a very narrow bridge, but the main thing is not to be afraid." —Rabbi Nachman of Breslov

Olam Ha-ba = World to come   Oneg Shabbat = Enjoyment/celebration of the Shabbat   Oy Vey! = Oh, no!

"O" IS FOR Orthodox,

Oy gevalt, and Oy vey

And whether Conservative, Reconstructionist, or Reform,

It's the "Hear O Israel" we all say.

THERE IS A PLACE FOR EVERYONE ALONG THE SPECTRUM OF JEWISH LIFE. There are three major movements—Reform, Conservative, and Orthodox—with no monolithic approach to Jewish life. Orthodox is the oldest and believes that the Torah was given by God to the Jewish people on Mount Sinai and every law should be followed precisely. Reform Judaism came along in the mid-19th century as a response to modernity and enlightenment. It believes that laws are for "guidance not governance" and the Torah was written by divinely inspired human beings. Conservative Judaism was founded as a response to Reform and sought to conserve some of the rituals that Reform rejected. Add Humanist and Reconstructionist to the mix, and we hope that each branch can strive to achieve a collective oneness that makes us, no matter what we are labeled, Klal Israel—unified Jewish people.

"After a certain number of years, our faces become our biographies." –Cynthia Ozick

"Keeping it all in the family"

Navah Perlman

Itzhak Perlman

Rami Perlman

Natalia Zukerman

Pinchas Zukerman

Arianna Zukerman

"P" IS FOR Perlman and Pinchas Zukerman,

Two of the best fiddlers on Earth.
And for Proverbs, Psalms, and Prophets—
Profound wisdom in every verse.

PSALMS ARE A COLLECTION OF 150 SACRED PRAYERS/POEMS—many attributed to King David—expressing a full range of Jewish faith and emotion. The book of Proverbs contains short, pithy statements that give advice on how to live ethically and morally. Many proverbs are attributed to King Solomon, one of the wisest people in history (even though he had 700 wives!). Prophets were spokespeople and messengers for God who challenged and admonished the Jewish people from the conquest of Canaan in 1200 BCE to the destruction of the First Temple in 586 BCE. The role of the biblical prophet was to comfort the afflicted and to afflict the comfortable. The prophets demanded social justice for all and reminded people to repent from their evil ways and return to following God's commandments. The weekly reading of the prophets is called the *haftarah*.

"Fear of Adonai is the beginning of knowledge, but fools despise wisdom and instruction." —**Proverbs 1:7**

"Teach us to number our days so that we can attain a heart of wisdom." —**Psalm 90**

"Q" IS FOR

Questions

That we are encouraged to ask

And for beautiful Queen Esther

And her so unenviable tasks.

QUESTIONING IS AT THE VERY HEART OF JEWISH LIFE. Judaism not only stimulates questioning, it evokes questions more often than it provides answers. Judaism is unique among religions in its encouragement of questioning. Through study, we interpret and reinterpret, amend and expand, as we constantly explore and seek new and deeper understanding of every aspect of the multiple layers of our tradition and faith. A great rabbi once said, "When I pray, I talk with God; when I study, God talks to me." Even more than finding the answers…keep asking questions!

"God, I have time, I have plenty of time, all the time that you give me. The years of my life, the days of my life, the days of my years, the hours of my days, they are all mine. Mine to fill, quietly, calmly, but to fill completely, up to the brim." —Michel Quoist

"R" IS FOR

Ruth,

Who chose to become a Jew.
Then came Marilyn, Sammy, and Elizabeth Taylor,
Just to name a few.

RUTH WAS THE VERY FIRST JEW BY CHOICE. Alive during the time of the Judges, around 500 BCE, Ruth was

a woman of great humility and pride. She was fiercely loyal to her mother-in-law, Naomi, incredibly independent, strong, and courageous.

She chose of her own volition to become Jewish. Through relationships, Ruth saw that Judaism was a combination of faith and community.

A person who is not born Jewish may become a Jew at anytime by converting to Judaism. For more than 1,800 years, Judaism has accepted,

incorporated, and welcomed anyone *meshugah* enough to choose to lead a Jewish life.

"Wherever you go I will go. Wherever you lodge I will lodge. Your people shall be my people, your God my God." —Ruth 1:16

"S" IS FOR

Shabbat,

The day of solemn rest,
And for Spitz, Strauss, and Spielberg,
Who strove to be the best.

EVERY 168 HOURS, we are commanded to turn off all the distractions in our lives and focus on ourselves and our families. Just as God finished the work of creation in six days and rested on the seventh, each one of us must do the same. Shabbat, the Sabbath, from sundown Friday to sundown Saturday, is a 24-hour period each week that permits each person to connect with God, family, and community through meditation, prayer, rest, and enjoyment. Shabbat is a weekly "mini-vacation" from the busy world of space that allows enjoyment of the "paradise of time." Hang in there...Shabbat is coming!

"The vaccine worked." –Jonas Salk

"The greatest Jewish tradition is to laugh. The cornerstone of Jewish survival has always been to find humor in life and in ourselves." –Jerry Seinfeld

Tallit = Prayershawl   **T'filah** = Prayer   **T'shuvah** = Return (repair yourself)   **Tzaddik** = Righteous person

"T" IS FOR

Tzedakah,

The righteous act of giving.
Commanded in the Torah,
It adds meaning to our living.

TORAH LITERALLY MEANS TEACHING. Torah is the Jewish peoples' most-cherished possession. Torah is read over and over, for everything is included in it. Torah contains the history, the laws, the traditions, and the stories of our people from the creation of the world until this very moment. Torah is always evolving and teaches us to love God and partner with God in *tikkun olam*, the continuous repair of our world. Torah is not just something we study and Tzedakah is not just something we do; they both transform us in the process. Torah is our always growing and blossoming tree of life, a tree with deep roots and wide branches.

"It is not our duty to complete the work, but neither are we free to abstain from it." —**Rabbi Tarfon**

"Who is wise?...One who learns from all people." —**Talmud**   "Take your shoes off....you're on holy ground." —**Craig Taubman**

Is what to look for

Inside the tiny "O."

If what you serve on isn't kosher,

Then off to the mikvah you will go.

KASHRUT (or keeping kosher) refers to the system of laws that outline what Jewish people can and cannot eat. The laws of kashrut evolved out of the Torah from the verse, "You shall not boil a kid in its mother's milk." Kosher certification agencies examine the ingredients used to make food, supervise the process by which the food is prepared, and inspect the processing facilities to make sure that proper standards are maintained. In 1923 the OU—Orthodox Union—declared that Heinz Vegetarian Beans would be the first American product to display the OU symbol. Now there are many other symbols that deem a product kosher. Keeping kosher is a wonderful way to think about your Jewishness every time you put food in your mouth.

"I think Yitzchak Rabin takes his place alongside David Ben Gurion as one of the two great Jews of the century. He soared. I think it was almost biblical, how the team—Rabin as a warrior and Peres as a poet—the two of them together made peace." —Leon Uris

Vey Is Mire = A cry of agony   Viddui = Confessional prayer   Vilde Chaya = Wild animal or wild person

"V" IS FOR

Vaudeville,

Where so many comics started.

Larry, Moe, Curly, Uncle Miltie—
They help us stay light-hearted.

BEGINNING WITH VAUDEVILLE and continuing through radio, stand-up comedy, film, and television, a high percentage of comedians have been Jewish. Laughter has always been a huge part of the Jewish experience. Woody Allen, Milton Berle, the Three Stooges, Jack Benny, Mel Brooks, Adam Sandler, George Burns, the Marx Brothers, and so many more Jewish comedians have made us laugh. The Jewish humor tradition (which goes all the way back to the Torah), a healthy dose of self-deprecation, and an instinct for self-preservation blended together and helped Jews flourish in the fertile new field of entertainment. Throughout our history, it has been said, "When it hurts too much to cry...we laugh."

"The goal of redemption is the redemption of truth." –Vilna Gaon

"W" IS FOR

Erich Weitz,

Known to us as Harry Houdini.
Elie Wiesel and Henry Winkler
Are also know to wear a "beanie."

THE WESTERN WALL IN JERUSALEM is the retaining wall built by King Herod surrounding the Temple Mount, the site of the First Temple, the Second Temple, and Mount Moriah, the very spot where Abraham almost sacrificed his son Isaac. Tradition teaches it is the place where the creation of the world took place, from the foundation stone at its peak. The Kotel or Western Wall became the most sacred spot in Jewish religious and national consciousness for it is the closest one could get to the Holy of the Holies. It is a symbol of hope, restoration, and return. As the popular Israeli folk song states, "There are humans with hearts of stone and then there are stones with human hearts." The 2,000-year-old stones of the Western Wall are a living tribute to the strength and resiliency of the Jewish people.

"Hope is like peace. It is not a gift from God. It is a gift we can only give to one another." —Elie Wiesel

X **Commandments** = **I God** **II Idols** **III Blasphemy** **IV Sabbath** **V Parents** **VI Murder**

VII Adultery **VIII Theft** **IX Perjury** **X Coveting** (Remember, these are not multiple choice.)

"X" IS FOR X-Men

Superheroes of comics, movies, and TV.
Created by Jacob Kurtzberg and Stanley Lieber...
Oops! Jack Kirby and Stan Lee.

FROM X-MEN TO SUPERMAN, Jews have built the comic book industry from the ground up, and the influence of

Jewish writers, artists, cartoonists, and editors continues to be felt to this day in arenas like comics, art, and music. Beginning in 1961, Stan

Lee and Jack Kirby created or co-created many classic characters, including Spider-Man, the Hulk, Thor, Iron Man, and X-Men. Through

these superheroes, Kirby and Lee were able to highlight a group of super-powered mutants who desperately tried to help the people who

feared and loathed them because they were different. Sometimes art imitates life, and through pictures and comics Jews have found yet

another way to overcome division and hatred. Like Moses, who was separated from his family and sent down the Nile River in a basket, 3,300

years later Superman was placed in a spaceship and sent to Earth to save humanity.

Yalla = Get going   Yarmulka = Head covering   Yontif = Holiday   Yasher Koach = "Strength to you"

Yahrtzeit = The annual anniversary to remember someone's death   Yad = Hand/Torah pointer   Yichus = Family status

"Y" IS FOR

Yenta,

Who gossips day and night
And reports all through Yom Kippur
On who stopped to get a bite.

YOM KIPPUR, the Day of Atonement, is considered the holiest of all the holidays, the Sabbath of Sabbaths. It is a day of individual and communal forgiveness. We all at some time or another "miss the mark." Yom Kippur is the renewal of our relationship with God. By fasting, practicing self-sacrifice, and spending the entire day in prayer we confess our sins as individuals and as a community and begin our new year with a fresh, clean slate.

"Each and every child brings their own blessing into the world." —Yiddish proverb

"Can God be God if God can only be worshipped in one way?" —Rabbi Yitzhak Yaakov (the Seer of Lublin)

Zachor = Remember   Zohar = Radiance (mystical book that is core text of Kabbalah)

Zayde and Bubbe = Grandfather and grandmother (Can't forget them!)

"Z" IS FOR THE Zohar,

Madonna's recent passion.
The mystic Kabbalah
May be Hollywood's latest fashion.

MYSTICISM AND MYSTICAL EXPERIENCES have been a part of Judaism since the earliest days. The Torah contains many stories of mystical experiences, from visitations by angels to prophetic dreams and visions. The Zohar, a book of mystery and splendor written by Rabbi Shimon Bar Yochai while he spent 13 years hiding in a cave during the second century CE, was revealed to Rabbi Moshe de Leon in Spain in the 13th century. The Zohar serves as the foundation for the explosion of mysticism and *Kabbalah* that would take place starting in Safed, the northern part of Israel, in the 16th century, and continuing on to Hollywood today. In the Zohar, we learn that every teaching has four different levels of understanding: the simple meaning; the implied meaning or hint; the homiletical or moral meaning; and the hidden mysterious and mystical meaning. These are represented in Hebrew by the words *P'shat, Remez, Drash,* and *Sod.* The first letters of these four words spell PaRDeS, meaning "orchard"—a beautiful garden to walk through trying to understand all the wonderful teachings our religion offers.

"When I pass from this world and stand before the heavenly tribunal, they will not ask me, 'Zusha, why were you not Moses or Abraham?' They will ask me, 'Zusha, why were you not Zusha?'" —Reb Zusha of Hanipoli

So that's our Jewish Alphabet (Aleph-Bet)
Filled with pride from A to Z.
With chutzpah, wisdom, patience, and grace,
That's how we came to be.

No part of this publication may be reproduced, stored in a retrieval system, or transmitted in any form by any means, electronic, mechanical, photocopying, or otherwise, without the prior written permission of the publisher, Triumph Books, 542 S. Dearborn Street, Suite 750, Chicago, Illinois 60605.
Triumph Books and colophon are registered trademarks of Random House, Inc.

This book is available in quantity at special discounts for your group or organization. For further information, contact:

Triumph Books
542 South Dearborn Street
Suite 750
Chicago, Illinois 60605
312. 939. 3330
Fax 312. 663. 3557

Printed in China
ISBN 978–1–60078–403–3

Todah Rabbah to Ben and Noah, Susan Klingman, Bob Moss, Mitch Rogatz, Julie Simon, Julie Stark, and of course the wonderful family at Am Shalom.